For all the animals in the tropical seas.
And in memory of my Granny—J.B.
For Isaac—K.B.

A Raspberry Book
Art direction & cover design: Sidonie Beresford-Browne
Design: Nicky Scott
Author: Jane Burnard
Editors: Nicola Edwards and Tracey Turner
Illustration: Kendra Binney
Consultant: Paul Lawston

KINGFISHER
LONDON & NEW YORK

Text and design copyright © Raspberry Books Ltd. 2023
First published 2023 in the United States by Kingfisher,
120 Broadway, New York, NY 10271
Kingfisher is an imprint of
Macmillan Children's Books, London

Distributed in the U.S. and Canada by Macmillan,
120 Broadway, New York, NY 10271

EU representative: 1st Floor, The Liffey Trust Centre,
117-126 Sheriff Street Upper, Dublin 1 D01 YC43

Library of Congress Cataloging-in-Publication Data has been applied for.

ISBN 978-0-7534-7847-9

Kingfisher books are available for special promotions and premiums.
For details contact: Special Markets Department, Macmillan, 120 Broadway,
New York, NY 10271

For more information, please visit
www.kingfisherbooks.com

Printed in China
1 3 5 7 9 8 6 4 2
1TR/1222/RV/WKT/140MA

ANIMAL LIFE IN TROPICAL SEAS

A Coral Reef Story

WRITTEN BY
JANE BURNARD

ILLUSTRATED BY
KENDRA BINNEY

KINGFISHER
LONDON & NEW YORK

HUMPBACK WHALE

BARRACUDA

SILVERSIDES

CORAL GROUPER

MORAY EEL

SEA GOLDIES

PORCUPINE FISH

VEINED OCTOPUS

GREEN TURTLE

CONVICT TANGS

CLOWN FISH

This is a
CORAL REEF.

A living, limestone necklace beneath
the sea, built over thousands of years
by billions of tiny creatures.

It is multicolored, ever-changing,
and full of animals. They are
made for this place, and it
is made for them.

CARPET ANEMONE

LAGOON

HERMIT CRAB

TIMOR WRASSE

LOBSTERS

CLEANER
SHRIMP

GREENTHROAT
PARROTFISH

SPOT-TAIL
BUTTERFLY FISH

BABY STARBURST
CORAL

BLUE DAMSELFISH

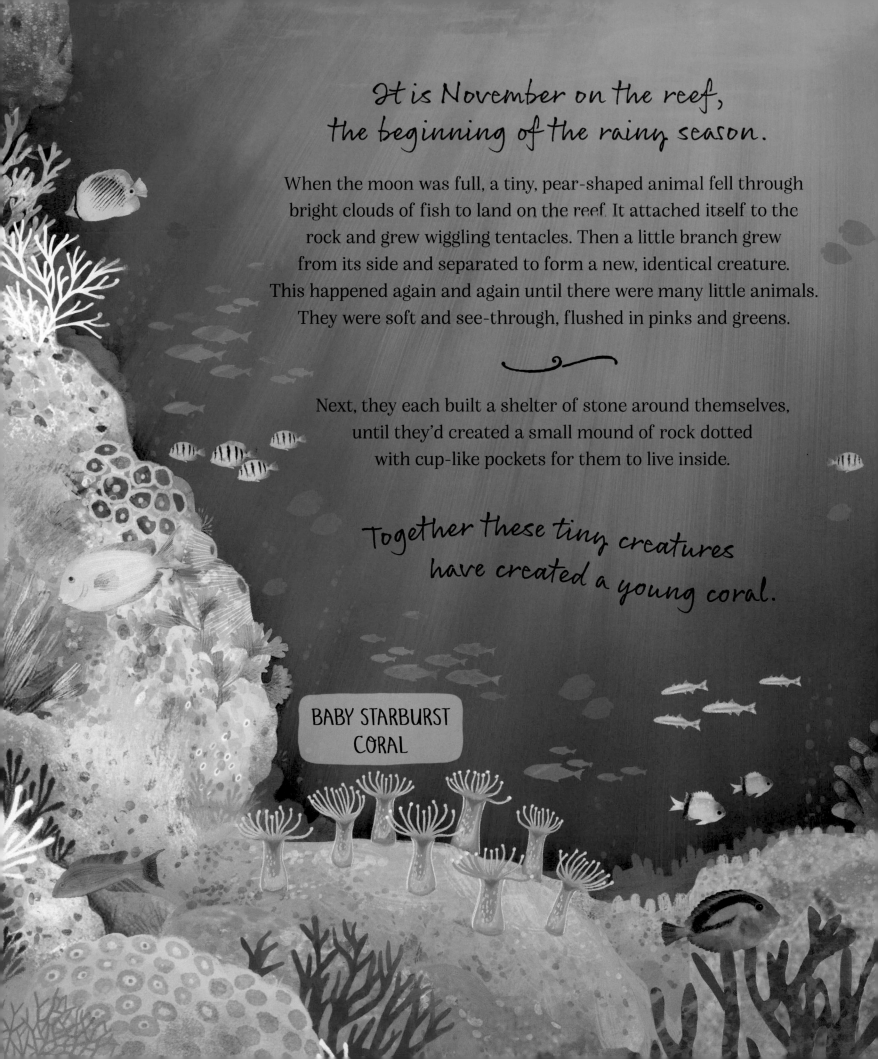

It is November on the reef,
the beginning of the rainy season.

When the moon was full, a tiny, pear-shaped animal fell through
bright clouds of fish to land on the reef. It attached itself to the
rock and grew wiggling tentacles. Then a little branch grew
from its side and separated to form a new, identical creature.
This happened again and again until there were many little animals.
They were soft and see-through, flushed in pinks and greens.

Next, they each built a shelter of stone around themselves,
until they'd created a small mound of rock dotted
with cup-like pockets for them to live inside.

Together these tiny creatures
have created a young coral.

BABY STARBURST
CORAL

Around it, other corals of all shapes and
sizes soar and spread. Every one of them
has been built by tiny creatures too.

But there are many dangers
on the bustling reef. The young coral may be
overgrown by algae or eaten by this
SPOT-TAIL BUTTERFLY FISH.

The animals that build corals are called POLYPS.
Tiny plant cells inside their bodies use the
sun's light to make food and energy, which the
polyps use to create limestone from minerals
in sea water. They also catch food with their
tentacles, which are lined with stinging cells.

CORAL REEFS are collections of
many types of stony corals.
The coral just beginning to grow is
a STARBURST CORAL. Tropical
coral reefs teem with wildlife.

Sun pours down through warm,
shallow water that's as clear and blue as mountain air.
Waves break gently on the reef's ridge.

Further along the curve of the reef, a pair of
spot-tail butterfly fish peck out polyps on a patch of
coral. Their yellow flanks signal like flags: this is our
coral patch; these are our polyps.

Around them, **BLUE DAMSELFISH** flit
about like little neon sparks. One of them
nibbles at the algae that forms a thin, green
coat over the coral, and the butterfly fish
dart over to chase it off.

A gang of **GREENTHROAT PARROTFISH** appear, cruising slowly over the reef like a herd of cows. They eat algae too. Ignoring the fluttering butterfly fish, they drop down to munch and scrape at the coral with strong, beak-like teeth, swallowing

algae, polyps, stone, and all.

Like many reef fish, SPOT-TAIL BUTTERFLY FISH have flat, disk-like bodies, which means they can turn quickly to escape from predators and fit into narrow cracks in the reef. They are polyp eaters and fiercely territorial. They tend to live alone—until they find a mate and stay with them for life.

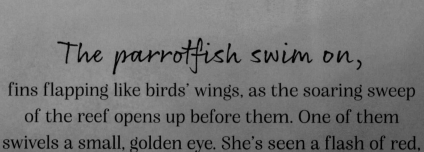

The parrotfish swim on,

fins flapping like birds' wings, as the soaring sweep
of the reef opens up before them. One of them
swivels a small, golden eye. She's seen a flash of red,
a stripe of white, on the seafloor below.

Dropping down

to land on the ocean floor,
she holds herself very still. A tiny,
bright-eyed **CLEANER SHRIMP** is
waving its antennae in a special signal.
The parrotfish flushes darker in reply
—she's telling it she won't eat it.

PARROTFISH teeth are designed for scraping or biting hard coral.
The stone is digested and pooped out as sand, which forms white beaches and
helps hold the reef together, making it stronger. A single parrotfish can produce
half a ton of sand a year. The scratches and scars that parrotfish leave on coral
surfaces make room for new corals and other organisms to settle and grow.

Then the cleaner shrimp scampers swiftly into the fish's open gills, riffling through them to eat harmful parasites and nibble off old skin.

The shrimp gets a tasty meal, and the parrotfish gets a good cleaning. When the cleaning session is over, the parrotfish lifts in a puff of white sand, flapping to rejoin her flock.

CLEANER SHRIMP set up "cleaning stations" near their homes, signaling to fish with their antennae. They eat the parasites, fungus, and dead flesh that make fish unhealthy. Even large predators like moray eels let them clean inside their mouths and gills without harming them.

Time passes. It's February now, a time of storms.

Dark clouds roll across the sky, blotting out the sun. The cleaner shrimp emerges, delicate antennae twitching. It senses a change in the water, which is colder, darker, unsettled. Lightning flashes and thunder rumbles, and the shrimp scampers back into its cave.

Now rain and strong winds lash the water above.

Powerful waves heave and crash against the ridge of the reef.

Beneath the surface,

swirling ocean swells whip up sand. Small fish spin helplessly in currents, while others cower in coral crevices. Fragile pieces of branched corals, broken by waves, come tinkling down the reef's slope.

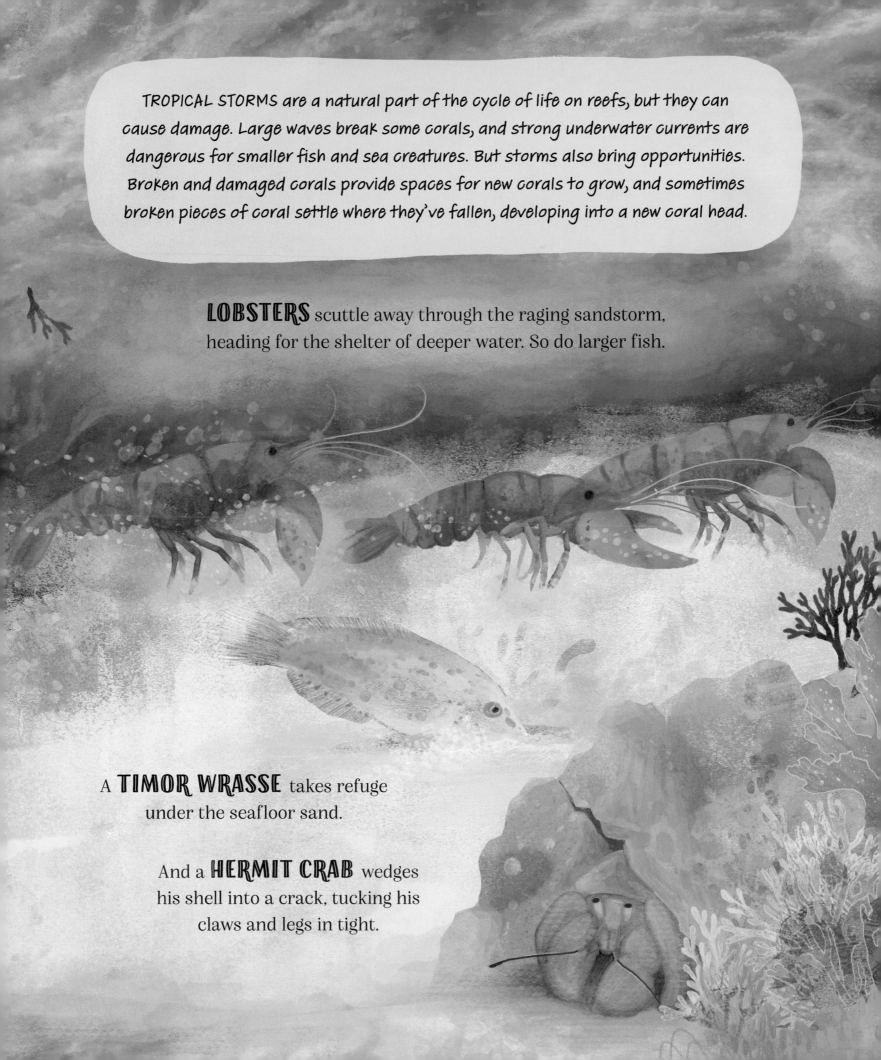

TROPICAL STORMS are a natural part of the cycle of life on reefs, but they can cause damage. Large waves break some corals, and strong underwater currents are dangerous for smaller fish and sea creatures. But storms also bring opportunities. Broken and damaged corals provide spaces for new corals to grow, and sometimes broken pieces of coral settle where they've fallen, developing into a new coral head.

LOBSTERS scuttle away through the raging sandstorm, heading for the shelter of deeper water. So do larger fish.

A **TIMOR WRASSE** takes refuge under the seafloor sand.

And a **HERMIT CRAB** wedges his shell into a crack, tucking his claws and legs in tight.

The storm has passed.

It has coated the reef in fine, white sand and left behind an empty shell.

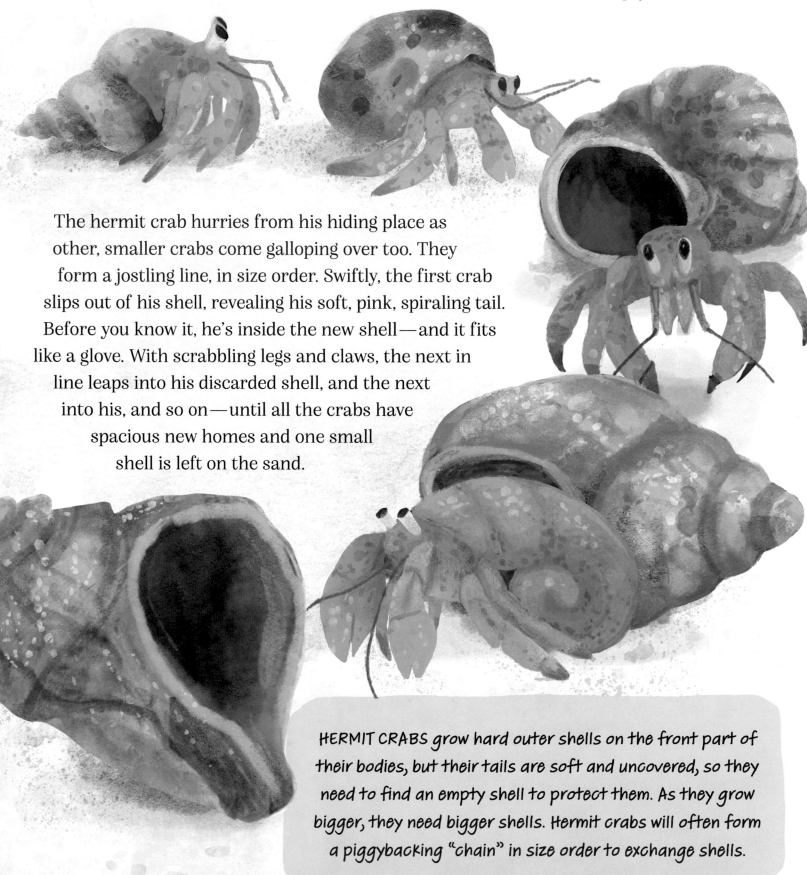

The hermit crab hurries from his hiding place as other, smaller crabs come galloping over too. They form a jostling line, in size order. Swiftly, the first crab slips out of his shell, revealing his soft, pink, spiraling tail. Before you know it, he's inside the new shell—and it fits like a glove. With scrabbling legs and claws, the next in line leaps into his discarded shell, and the next into his, and so on—until all the crabs have spacious new homes and one small shell is left on the sand.

HERMIT CRABS grow hard outer shells on the front part of their bodies, but their tails are soft and uncovered, so they need to find an empty shell to protect them. As they grow bigger, they need bigger shells. Hermit crabs will often form a piggybacking "chain" in size order to exchange shells.

In the swirling tentacles of a **CARPET ANEMONE**,
a female **CLOWN FISH**, the leader of the group, is getting ready to lay her eggs.
The others are rushing around, showing her how useful they are. They blow
the storm's sand off the anemone, vacuum up debris,
and carefully carry away seaweed.

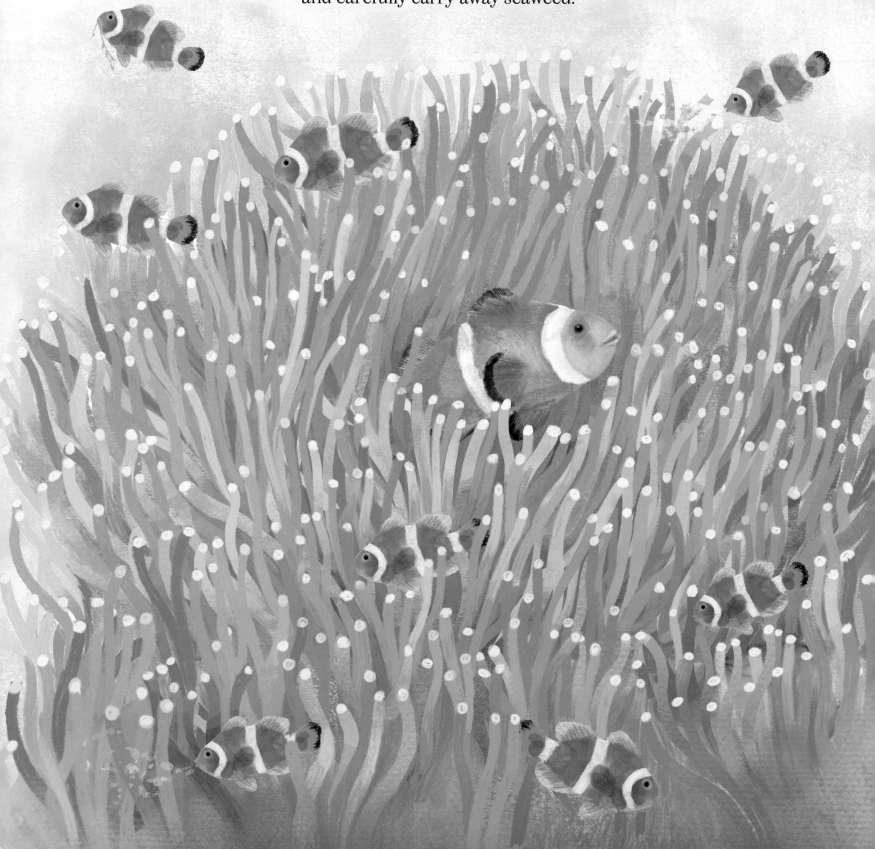

Soon the big day arrives.

The female clown fish lays row upon row of long, golden eggs, and now the father—the largest male in the group—takes charge of the eggs, fanning them devotedly and driving off unwelcome guests.

Before long, two silvery eyes appear

in each carefully tended egg. A week later, just after dusk and under a full moon, they hatch.

Hundreds of tiny

clown fish, no bigger than fleas, go spiraling upward to seek their fortunes in the open ocean. In time, when they're larger and tougher, some will return to the reef.

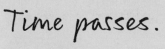

Time passes.

It's July—the middle of the dry season.

The ring of the reef pulses with life, and with constant sound.

Shrimp sizzle and pop. Clown fish chirp. Schools of
grazing **CONVICT TANGS** snip-snip-snip. But the loudest
sound, the most haunting, mysterious, and strange, is the
HUMPBACK WHALE'S soaring song.

CLOWN FISH live within anemones, which are simple animals rather like
coral polyps, with a base, a central mouth, and stinging tentacles. Mucus on
a clown fish's skin protects it from these stings. Anemones keep clown fish
safe from predators and provide food scraps from the prey they sting, while
clown fish keep the anemone clean of debris and drive off intruders.

The humpback whales have returned. They have traveled long, danger-filled distances to gather in the reef's sun-warmed shallows.

They are here to mate and to give birth.

A huge male hangs in the water, filling the sea with song. Others float in from out of the blue. They turn long fins to twist slowly in the water, revealing white, lined undersides and calm, intelligent eyes.

With a thrust of their powerful tails they propel themselves headfirst from the water, turn joyfully in the air, and fall backward with a huge splash.

Full-grown HUMPBACK WHALES are as big as buses and can live for more than 50 years. Every year, they travel thousands of miles from summer feeding grounds in the cold waters of the polar regions to tropical reefs, to give birth and to mate. Male humpbacks sing echoing songs that can travel for many miles across the ocean.

A mother and
her newborn calf drift
gently together, the
calf mirroring her slow
movements, safe beneath the
wing of her fin. While the big males sing,
the calf whispers soft squeaks.

Beneath them, a writhing ball
of **SILVERSIDES** speeds through
the water, pursued by deadly
BARRACUDA.

Barracuda slice through the sea like shining steel rockets, driving fish before them in a rushing, silver cloud that twists and turns and flashes as it catches the sun's light. The barracuda are herding the silversides around the curve of the reef.

Now they turn, suddenly, to drive them into the rocks and break them up among the corals.

The silverside cloud hits the reef slope and explodes, with single silversides shooting off in all directions. Then the barracuda strike at their prey, mouths open, snapping up fish.

Smelling blood, a **CORAL GROUPER** twists her tail and grabs at a fleeing silverside. But she's not fast enough, and it streaks away.

The next moment,

the silversides and the barracuda have vanished. All that's left is a spray of silver scales, flashing on their way to the seafloor.

BARRACUDA are deadly predators. Their long, slender shape makes them very fast swimmers, capable of short bursts as fast as Usain Bolt! The silversides are "schooling" here—gathering together to try to confuse their predators, making it hard for them to focus on just one fish. Barracuda school too, when they're chased by sharks.

Days later, the grouper is still hungry.
So she sets off for a cave she knows. Hovering
outside it, she shakes her head vigorously,
shimmying her body.

Slowly, very slowly, a head appears.
It eyes the grouper and its mouth
sags open, revealing rows of sharp
teeth. It's a **MORAY EEL.**

As he slips from his cave, his long, ribbon-like
tail seems to go on forever. Side by side, they
glide upward, the eel snaking around rocks,
the grouper leading the way.

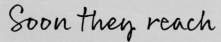

Soon they reach

a maze of coral heads and the grouper does a headstand, shaking her head again.

The eel gets the message and dives into a narrow gap in the rocks. As soon as his tail disappears, the grouper flits around the coral to block the escape route.

She's rewarded with a meal of fleeing **SEA GOLDIES.**

CORAL GROUPERS mostly eat small fish. Their bodies aren't slim and flexible enough to follow fish into the narrow cracks and crevices of coral reefs, so sometimes they team up with moray eels. They use signals to invite them to hunt and to point out prey. Sometimes the eel ends up with a meal, and sometimes the grouper does.

Meanwhile, the eel's
powerful sense of smell tells
him there's something tasty lurking
among the corals. But his eyesight is poor.
When a **PORCUPINE FISH** swims by,
drawn by the smaller fish,

he lunges blindly at it.

MORAY EELS are fearsome ambush predators with two sets of jaws—
one in the back of their throat, which they can extend forward to
grab hold of prey. They have poor eyesight, so they depend on their
strong sense of smell when hunting, which often takes place at night.

Sucking in water, the porcupine fish balloons to twice
its size, sharp spines jabbing outward. The moray eel
spits it out, and the fish bounces away,

upside down.

Frustrated, the eel
heads back to his cave.
He'll hunt again tonight,
under cover of darkness.

A little outcrop on the coral shifts, flushes crimson,
then speeds away, eight long arms trailing neatly behind.
It's a **VEINED OCTOPUS.**

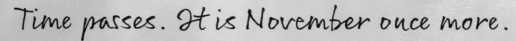

Time passes. It is November once more.

A **GREEN TURTLE** glides gracefully above a shallow, sandy alcove. Her amber shell glows, and the light outlines on her patterned skin shine bright against the clean white sand and deep blue water.

She's enjoying the warmth of the sun on her back. Her dark, oval eyes slowly blink. It's been a long time. She's spent twenty years cruising the open ocean, and now she's returning to the beach

where she hatched.

On the seafloor sand

lies a coconut shell. As the turtle passes, it cracks in half. Eyes appear, to check the coast is clear.

Then elegant tentacles, lined with white suckers, lift the lid, and the veined octopus steps out of his home and tip-tentacles away, the shell halves tucked neatly under his arms.

Octopuses are masters of disguise, able to mold their boneless bodies into different shapes and to change the texture and color of their skin to match their surroundings. The VEINED OCTOPUS does even better. It lives in sandy places, where there's not much cover. So it uses coconut and clam shells to make shelters to hide in and dens from which to ambush prey.

It is night, and a full moon shines

on the green turtle as she pulls herself up the beach, digs
a hole with her flippers, and lays ninety precious eggs.

GREEN TURTLES' light, streamlined shells (called carapaces) and powerful
flippers make them great swimmers, able to spend years in the open sea. Male
turtles spend their whole lives at sea, but females, once they're mature, return
every two to four years to the beach where they hatched, to lay eggs.

The moon's reflection shimmers down through the water too. A year has passed, and the reef has come full circle. The **STARBURST CORAL'S** glowing polyps sway in the current. It has survived all the reef's dangers. It has grown and flourished.

The reef is very quiet. As if it is waiting.

Then it begins. All across the reef, countless millions of coral polyps swell in readiness. Then, from every one, pops a tiny, round package—a precious bundle of eggs and sperm—until the water is a snowstorm of orange, pink, red, and yellow. Each one is full of potential new lives, lifting hopefully from the coral.

The CORAL POLYPS' mass release of eggs and sperm happens once a year following a full moon. Fertilized eggs develop into baby polyps, which are driven by tides and currents to different parts of the reef, or to other reefs. Some, like the young starburst, settle there and grow.

Soon, a tiny, pear-shaped animal, not yet fully formed, will fall through bright clouds of fish to land once more on a reef . . .

This is a CORAL REEF.

A living, limestone necklace beneath the sea, built over thousands of years by billions of tiny creatures.

It is multicolored, ever-changing, and full of animals. They are made for this place, and it is made for them.